8/09

BKW

Whales and Dolphins Up Close

NARWHAL WHALES

UP CLOSE

by **Jody Sullivan Rake**

Consultant:
Deborah Nuzzolo
Education Manager
SeaWorld, San Diego

Capstone
press®

Mankato, Minnesota

First Facts is published by Capstone Press,
151 Good Counsel Drive, P.O. Box 669, Mankato, Minnesota 56002.
www.capstonepress.com

Library of Congress Cataloging-in-Publication Data
Rake, Jody Sullivan.
    Narwhal whales up close / by Jody Sullivan Rake.
    p. cm. — (First facts. Whales and dolphins up close)
    Includes bibliographical references and index.
    Summary: "Presents an up-close look at narwhal whales, including their body
features, habitat, and life cycle" — Provided by publisher.
    ISBN-13: 978-1-4296-2266-0 (hardcover)
    ISBN-10: 1-4296-2266-0 (hardcover)
    1. Narwhal — Juvenile literature. I. Title.
QL737.C433R356 2009
599.5'43 — dc22   2008030106

Editorial Credits
Christine Peterson, editor; Renée T. Doyle, designer; Wanda Winch, photo researcher

Photo Credits
Alamy/Bryan & Cherry Alexander Photography, 21
Getty Images Inc./Minden Pictures/Flip Nicklin, 8 (inset), 14 (inset), 17; National
      Geographic/Paul Nicklen, 1, 5, 7 (bottom right), 13 (bottom right), 14, 20, cover
Minden Pictures/Flip Nicklin, 8–9, 11, 12–13
SeaPics.com/Doc White, 18; Saul Gonor, 6–7
Shutterstock/DeepGreen, 2, 3, 24; Timmary, (background throughout)

1 2 3 4 5 6 14 13 12 11 10 09

TABLE OF CONTENTS

Unicorns of the Sea

Do whales really have **tusks**? You bet. Narwhal whales do. These whales are called the "unicorns of the sea." These ocean animals are also mammals. Mammals breathe air, have warm bodies, and give birth to live young.

Long, pointed tusks set narwhals apart from other whales. This twisted, rough tooth grows out of its mouth. A tusk can grow to 9 feet (2.7 meters). That's more than half the length of a narwhal's body.

tusk — a long, pointed tooth

Narwhal Shapes

Narwhals are shaped like sausages. Males can weigh up to 3,500 pounds (1,600 kilograms). Females weigh less. Up to one-third of a narwhal's weight comes from blubber. This thick layer of fat keeps them warm in the icy water.

A blowhole helps narwhals breathe. A strong flap opens the blowhole above water. It closes tightly in water.

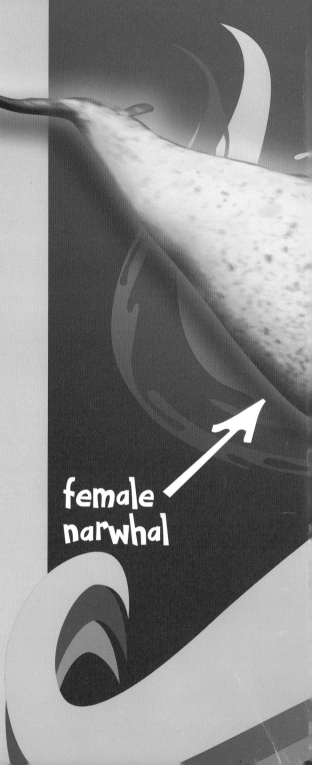

female narwhal

Tusks

Only male narwhals have tusks. No one knows for sure what the tusk is for. Some scientists think male narwhals fight with their tusks like swords. Others think it is just a male feature, like a lion's mane.

tusk

fluke — the wide,
flat end of a whale's tail

8

fluke

Strong Swimmers

Narwhals' smooth bodies are built to swim through icy water. Their tail **flukes** are shaped like fans. Narwhals flip their flukes up and down to swim. Narwhals have two flippers that look like paddles.

Narwhals sometimes look dead when they float belly up. That's why their name means "corpse whale."

Life in the Frozen North

Brrr! Narwhals live in icy **Arctic** waters. Most are found around Greenland and Canada's Baffin Island.

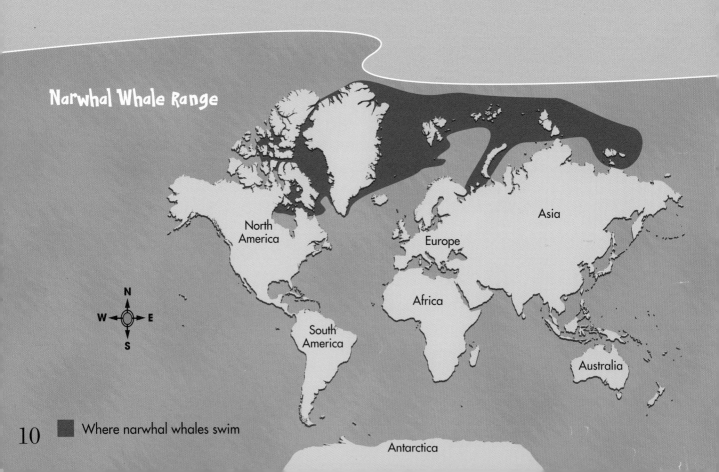

Narwhal Whale Range

North America

South America

Europe

Africa

Asia

Australia

Antarctica

N
W E
S

Where narwhal whales swim

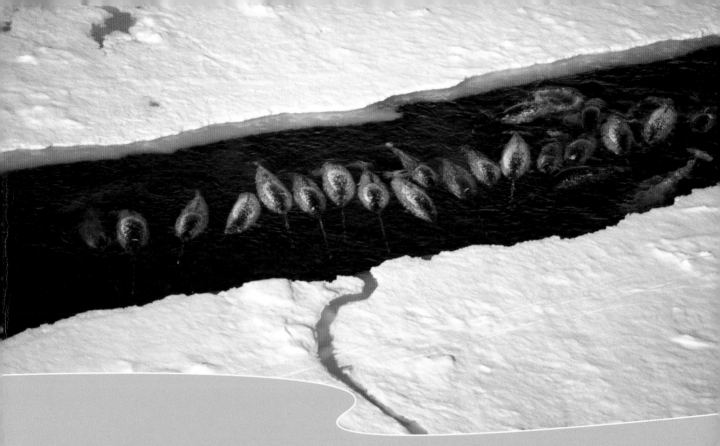

The area around the North Pole is frozen all year long. Some ice melts in the summer. Narwhals stay at the edge of this ice. In winter, they move into deeper waters.

Arctic — the area near the North Pole

Safety in Numbers

Narwhals live in groups to stay safe from **predators**. A group may have 20 to 30 narwhals. A large group may have males and females of all ages. Smaller groups may have just males or females with young.

predator — an animal that hunts other animals for food
plankton — tiny plants and animals that drift or float in water

Cool Colors

Narwhals are darker on top and lighter on their bellies. This coloring helps them hide from predators like killer whales. Most adults are spotted. Their spots make them look like **plankton**.

13

Finding Food

Narwhals are big, but their food is small. They eat mainly Arctic cod, squid, and shrimp. Narwhals hunt in deep bays. They dive to find **prey** near the bottom of the bay.

Narwhals have no teeth for grabbing food. Instead, they suck food into their mouths and swallow it whole.

prey — an animal hunted for food

15

Narwhal Life Cycle

Female narwhals give birth once every three years. Male and female narwhals mate in the spring. About 15 months later, a narwhal **calf** is born. At birth calves are 5 feet (1.5 meters) long. They weigh about 175 pounds (79 kilograms). Their smooth skin is usually gray.

calf — a baby whale

Life Cycle of a Narwhal Whale

Calf
A baby narwhal weighs 175 pounds (79 kilograms).

Mom and Baby

Young
At age 2, young narwhals care for themselves.

Adult
Adult male and female narwhals mate in spring.

Young Narwhals

Narwhal calves grow quickly drinking their mothers' rich milk. Calves stay close to their mothers. Their mothers keep them safe from killer whales and polar bears.

By age 2, young narwhals can care for themselves. Some narwhals stay with the same group. Others find a new group to join. Narwhals live at least 25 years.

Amazing but True!

All narwhals' tusks are twisted, like licorice. The twists go in the same direction. They turn in circles away from the narwhal's face. The tusk grows for a narwhal's whole life.

Like your teeth, the narwhal's tusk has some feeling. Their tusks can feel temperature change and movement in the water.

Narwhal Whales and People

Arctic natives hunt narwhals for food and for their tusks. Today more than 1,000 narwhals are hunted each year. Scientists believe this may be too many for narwhals to survive.

Changes people make to the earth also harm narwhals. Global climate change puts narwhals at risk. Losing so many narwhals makes it hard for this animal group to survive.

Glossary

Arctic (ARK-tik) — the area near the North Pole; the Arctic is cold and covered with ice.

calf (KAF) — a young whale or dolphin

fluke (FLOOK) — the wide, flat area at the end of a whale's tail

plankton (PLANGK-tuhn) — tiny plants and animals that drift or float in water

predator (PRED-uh-tur) — an animal that hunts other animals for food

prey (PREY) — an animal hunted by another animal for food

tusk (TUHSK) — a long, pointed tooth

Read More

Halfmann, Janet. *Narwhal Unicorn of the Sea.* Smithsonian Oceanic Collection. Norwalk, Conn.: Soundprints Division of Trudy Corporation, 2008.

Nicklin, Flip, and Linda Nicklin. *Face to Face With Whales.* Face to Face with Animals. Washington, D.C.: National Geographic, 2008.

Internet Sites

FactHound offers a safe, fun way to find educator-approved Internet sites related to this book.

Here's what you do:

1. Visit *www.facthound.com*
2. Choose your grade level.
3. Begin your search.

This book's ID number is 9781429622660.

FactHound will fetch the best sites for you!

Index